OUR PLANET:
EARTH

Contents

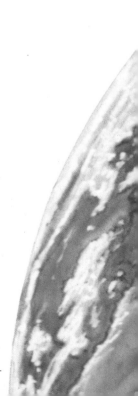

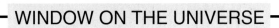

OUR PLANET: EARTH

Barron's Educational Series

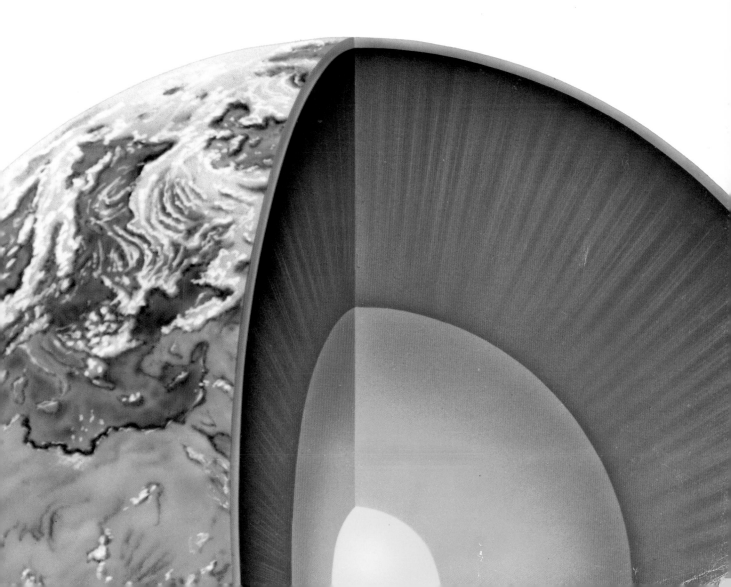

A planet called Earth

Our own planet, Earth, together with other planets, satellites, and numerous smaller bodies, forms part of the Solar System. The Sun, the central star of our Solar System, is just one among the billions of stars that make up our galaxy, the Milky Way. This galaxy is also just one of countless galaxies that fill our universe.

Earth differs from the rest of the planets in three important ways: First, here water exists in liquid form; moreover, water covers the greater part of the Earth's surface. Some satellites, and even Mars, have water in the form of ice on their surfaces, but at present no other body has liquid water. Second, Earth's **atmosphere** is largely composed of **oxygen**, while the atmospheres of Venus and Mars are made up mainly of **carbon dioxide** and those of the largest or *giant planets* (Jupiter, Saturn, Uranus, and Neptune) consist mostly of hydrogen. Third, and most importantly, life seems to be present only on Earth. Up to now, no form of life has been found anywhere else in the Solar System although the possibility of primitive forms of life existing on a satellite of one of the giant planets has not been completely ruled out.

Below: Earth is the third planet in order of distance from the Sun. The *terrestrial planets* (Mercury, Venus, Earth, and Mars) are the ones located nearest to the Sun. Further away are the four giant planets and tiny Pluto.

Bottom: The Moon is a very large satellite in relation to Earth. Its diameter is more than one-fourth the size of Earth's diameter.

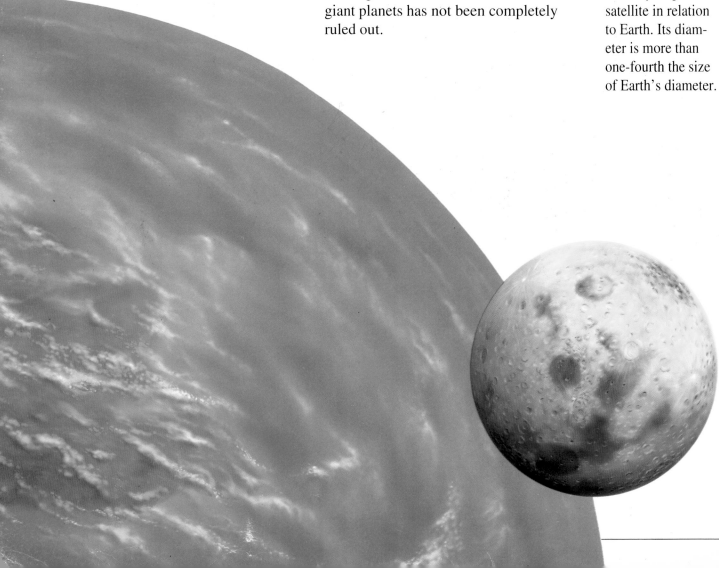

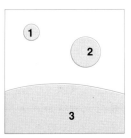

Below: Two types of planets revolve around the Sun ①, the central star of the Solar System. Earth ② is one of the four *terrestrial* planets, along with Mercury, Venus, and Mars. All of them are fairly small, are composed mainly of rock, and have very few satellites or none at all. On the other hand, the *giant planets* such as Jupiter ③, are much larger and mainly made up of gases. They are also surrounded by large families of satellites.

Movements of the Earth

Earth, like all the bodies in the Solar System, is trapped by the gravitational pull of the Sun. Because of this force, the Earth travels in an orbit around the Sun, taking a year to complete each trip. This journey around the Sun is one of the reasons for the changing seasons throughout the year. The distance from the Earth to the Sun varies very little along the orbit; it averages 93 million miles (150 million km). This distance is so great that the light of the Sun takes more than eight minutes to reach the Earth.

While orbiting around the Sun, the Earth also spins on its own axis, completing one revolution each day. This is why we have day and night. Since the Earth rotates toward the east, to us on Earth the Sun seems to move from east to west. Each morning we can see it rise above the eastern horizon. We then watch it reach its highest point in the sky toward the south at noon (when viewed from the Northern Hemisphere). Finally, we see it setting over the western horizon in the evening. At night we can also see an

apparent east-to-west movement of the whole night sky, that is, in the direction opposite that of the rotation of the Earth. The stars move in the same way as the Sun. Throughout the night, new stars appear over the eastern horizon and set over the western horizon.

Above: In the polar regions the Sun never sets entirely in summer. Near midnight it approaches the horizon, but without setting completely. This phenomenon is known as the *midnight sun*, visible from latitudes within the Arctic and Antarctic circles.

Right: The Sun does not always rise or set at the same point on the horizon. In summer it follows a higher path in the sky than in winter.

Below: At night we can see an apparent movement of the whole night sky, which turns in the opposite direction from that of the rotation of the Earth. If we look at the North Star in the Northern Hemisphere (the Earth's axis of rotation in space points toward this star), we can see how the stars turn all together around the North Star in a "counter-clockwise" (east to west) direction. There is no bright South Star in the Southern Hemisphere, but the stars seem to pivot, clockwise, around one particular point in the southern sky, called the *south celestial pole*.

The changing seasons

We are used to seeing how the seasons change throughout the year: spring, summer, autumn, winter.

There are two reasons why the seasons occur: the inclination of our Earth's axis and the movement of Earth around the Sun.

The north end of the axis of rotation of Earth points almost directly at the North Star. However, the Earth's axis is not perpendicular to the plane of its orbit around the Sun. So, while the Earth is traveling around the Sun, there is one particular moment in the year when the Sun reaches a high point above the Earth's equator. At another moment, six months later, the Sun is exactly the same distance below the equator. These two moments are called **solstices**. They occur around June 21 and December 21, and they mark the beginning of summer and winter. The **equinoxes**, which occur around March 21 and September 21, mark the beginning of the other two seasons, spring and autumn.

Below: The Earth at the beginning of summer in the Northern Hemisphere and winter in the Southern Hemisphere (*left*). Six months later, it will be winter in the Northern Hemisphere and summer in the Southern Hemisphere (*right*).

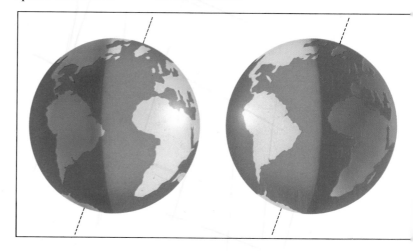

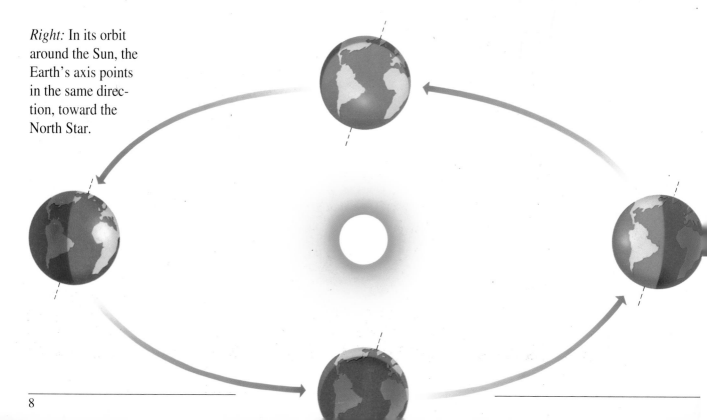

Right: In its orbit around the Sun, the Earth's axis points in the same direction, toward the North Star.

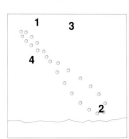

Below: This picture shows the position of the Sun at the same time in the morning every two weeks for a whole year. In summer ① the Sun is high, which means that the days are longer than the nights; in winter the opposite is true because the Sun is lower ②. Since the movement of the Earth around the Sun does not always follow an exact pattern, there are times in the year when the Sun appears to move forward slightly ③ and others when it hangs back ④ in its position. These two effects cause the Sun's apparent positions to trace a figure "8" called an *analemma*.

Formation of the Earth

The Earth came into existence along with the rest of the Solar System at the same time as the Sun was being formed. Some five billion years ago in our galaxy, a cloud of *intersteller matter* (the gas and dust between the stars) began to press together under its own gravitational pull.

In the center of the cloud the Sun condensed. The rest of the cloud created a flat disc that began to spin around the Sun and matter continued to gradually form into particles that collided with each other forming bodies, some as large as one-half mile (1 km) in diameter. The **core** of the Earth, formed from the collision of several of these bodies, attracted some of the matter near it. This is how ours and all the other planets and satellites were created. The whole process of the formation of the Sun and planets took several hundred million years, which is a very short time compared with the age of the Solar System.

That newly formed Earth was very different from the one we know today. The disintegration of accumulated radioactive matter and continuous bombardment from bodies falling on the Earth produced a fierce heat that caused the fusion of the interior of the planet. The most dense matter settled toward the center of the planet, forming a core of iron and nickel. At the same time, the lighter matter floated toward the surface, forming a **mantle** of molten rock made up of **silicates**. As the planet cooled, the surface crust of solid rock was formed, the rock that the ocean beds and the **continents** are made of.

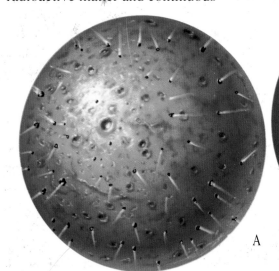

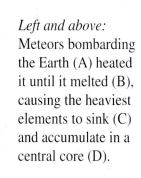

Left and above: Meteors bombarding the Earth (A) heated it until it melted (B), causing the heaviest elements to sink (C) and accumulate in a central core (D).

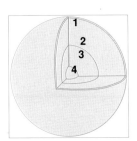

Below: Beneath the thin crust of the Earth ① there is a structure of layers that become progressively denser and hotter.

The mantle ② is made of molten rock, while the outer core holds the heavy elements, such as iron, in a liquid state ③. Within the

inner core ④ the iron is in a solid state because of the very high pressure the outer layers produce.

Earth is bombarded by meteorites

When the Solar System was young and the planets had only just formed, interplanetary space was littered with material that had not come together to make planets. Many bodies fell on the newly formed Earth, drawn by its gravitational pull. This continuous bombardment contributed to the heating and fusion of the Earth's matter in the first stages.

Now, interplanetary space is much cleaner. The bodies that still fall on the Earth are, in general, small particles of interplanetary dust that are swept along by the Earth in its journey around the Sun. These fragments enter the atmosphere at high speeds and, owing to the air friction, they become very hot and vaporize, forming a **meteor** or shooting star. If the body is large, part of it may survive its passage through the atmosphere and reach the ground. Then it is called a **meteorite**, a rock that has fallen from the sky. When these meteorites are really big, they may leave craters where they land on the Earth's surface. There are a few craters on Earth caused by meteorites.

Below: Meteorites that reach the Earth at high speeds can cause craters similar to those on the Moon. These areas are slightly sunken in relation to the surface around them.

Right: When a large meteorite falls, its impact can produce a crater like this one in Arizona. However, erosion can make these craters disappear in a few million years, a relatively short time compared with the age of the Earth.

Below: The space between the planets is not empty. Interplanetary debris of all sizes and shapes is found here: asteroids, comets, dust, and even gas. Most asteroids have accumulated in an area of the Solar System called the *asteroid belt*, which is located more or less between Mars and Jupiter. The gravitational influence of Jupiter, the largest planet of the Solar System, has prevented these bodies from coming together to form a planet.

The Earth's crust

The surface layer of the Earth is known as its **crust**. The crust's structure is very mixed. In the continental areas it is roughly 30 miles (50 km) thick, whereas under the oceans it is only about 4 miles (6 km) thick, that is, only about one-thousandth of the Earth's radius.

The crust and the mantle beneath it consist of rock made of silicon and other elements. In the mantle, the rock is molten because of the high temperatures, and is called magma. In the crust, on the other hand, the rock is solid. The crust is not rigid or immobile; rather, it is made up of large plates that support the continents as they float on the mantle. The currents of the magma in the mantle slowly push the continental plates around, causing **continental drift**. Where two continental plates collide, the crust folds and forms large mountain ranges.

The crust of the ocean bed often sinks deeply toward the mantle near the edges of the continents. The continual readjustments that are occurring in the lower part of the crust are often the cause of frequent **earthquakes** in these areas. The parts of the globe where earthquakes usually occur form a wide curve that takes in both shores of the Pacific Ocean from Chile, in South America, to Indonesia, to the north of Australia.

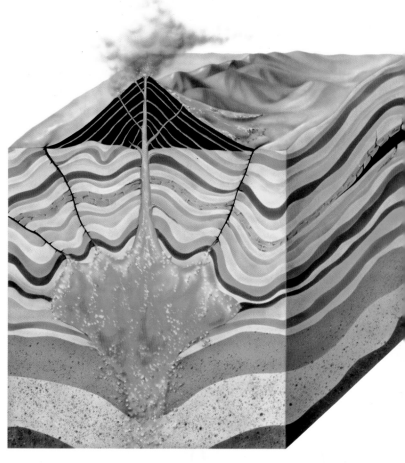

Above: When the molten rock, or magma, rises to the surface, volcanoes are created. The areas of the world that have a great deal of volcanic activity also tend to have frequent earthquakes.

Below: The volcanoes of Io, a satellite of Jupiter, propel sulfurous material to great heights.

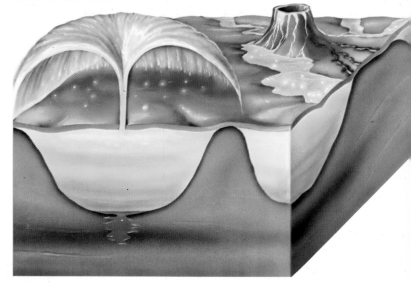

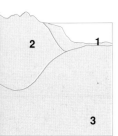

Below: The Earth's crust is much thinner at the bottom of the oceans ① than on the continents ②. The plates that support the continents "float" on the mantle ③ and move slowly around, pushed by the currents of magma. The folds in the crust produce mountain ranges. The highest mountains on Earth, the Himalayas, rise more than 5 miles (8 km) above sea level. They were formed when the plate containing the Indian subcontinent pushed against the asiatic plate.

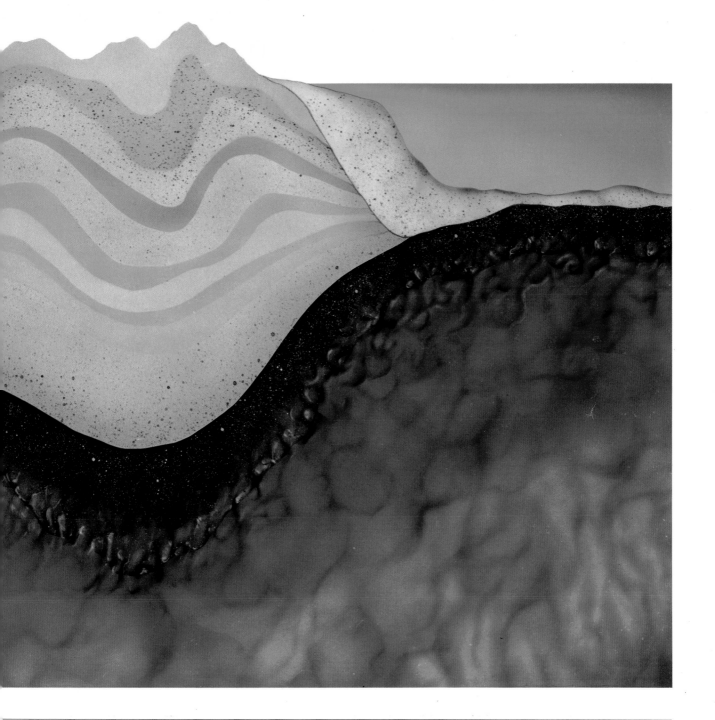

Earth's magnetism

The Earth has a fairly intense magnetic field. Think of it as a huge magnetized bar inside the Earth's core, but placed slightly off center and tilted with respect to the Earth's axis of rotation. The magnetic north pole of the Earth is near the geographic north pole, although they do not coincide. The distance between these two poles is in fact some 600 miles (1000 km). The same situation applies to the southern magnetic and geographic poles. A compass, which is simply a magnetized needle that can swing freely, points to the magnetic pole, and therefore indicates a northerly direction.

How did the Earth's magnetic field originate? For example, in an electromagnet, the magnetic field is produced by an electric current flowing through a wire coil. In the case of Earth, there are electric currents flowing through its metallic core, which you will recall is composed mainly of iron and nickel. Thus, the core acts like a giant electromagnet generating the electric current that results in the Earth's magnetic field.

The Earth's magnetic field extends toward space and interacts with charged particles from the Sun. The part of interplanetary space where the influence of the Earth's magnetism has a noticeable effect is called the **magnetosphere**. The charged particles that continuously stream from the Sun are deflected by the magnetic field when they reach the Earth's magnetosphere.

Below: The stream of charged particles in the **solar wind** are deflected by the Earth's magnetic field when they reach the Earth's magnetosphere. Most particles flow around the Earth, but some are trapped in two belt-like areas around the Earth known as the **Van Allen belts**. They contain a great number of highly charged particles.

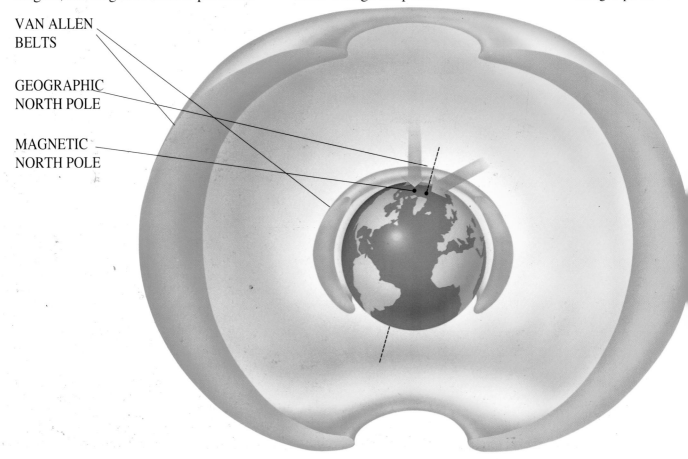

VAN ALLEN
BELTS

GEOGRAPHIC
NORTH POLE

MAGNETIC
NORTH POLE

Below: Some high-energy particles emitted by the Sun can reach the Earth's atmosphere in areas near the magnetic poles. When they strike the atmosphere, the atoms of atmospheric gas shimmer with brightly colored lights and can be seen high up in the sky. This is the *aurora,* or northern and southern lights, normally seen only in latitudes close to either pole.

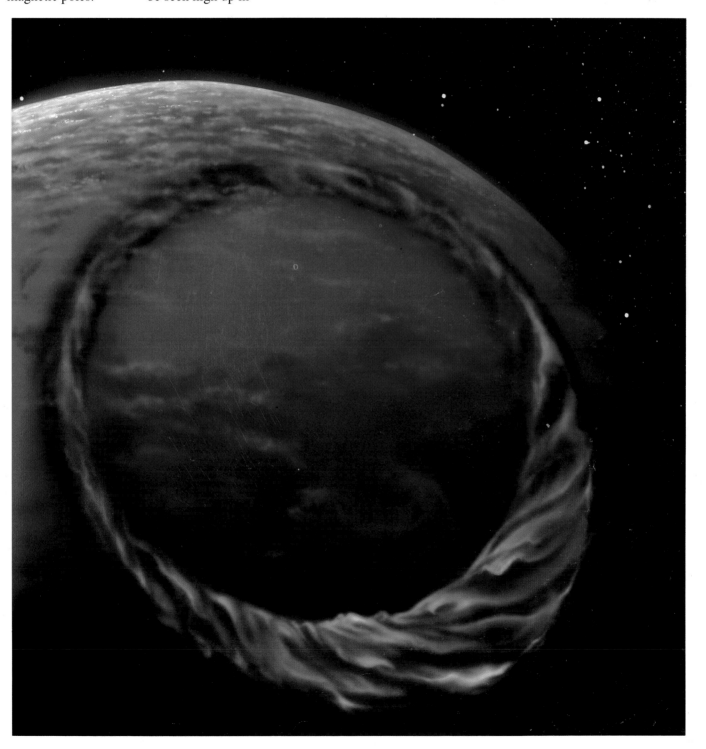

Formation of the Earth's atmosphere

The Earth is surrounded by a gaseous layer that we call the atmosphere.

Earth's present-day atmosphere is not at all like the original atmosphere that was formed at the same time as the planet. When the Sun was newly formed, the original layer of gases surrounding the planets near the Sun was completely swept away by an intense stream of particles emitted by the early Sun. Today's atmosphere is the result of intense volcanic action during the first phases of the Earth's evolution. The volcanoes threw up large quantities of carbon dioxide, steam, and other gases.

After cooling, the temperature on Earth was appropriate for water vapor to condense into liquid, and this is how the oceans were formed. A great deal of carbon dioxide was dissolved in the sea water. From there, it passed to the shells of uncountable generations of marine animals that fell to the seabed when they died. These sediments then turned into what are now limestone deposits.

The nitrogen in our atmosphere comes from ammonia-loaded gases given off by ancient volcanoes that was then decomposed by ultraviolet light from the Sun. The oxygen, on the other hand, resulted from the evolution of life on Earth. Green algae in the oceans, one of the first forms of life to appear, consumed carbon dioxide from the atmosphere and produced a large quantity of oxygen.

Left: Earth's atmosphere consists mainly of nitrogen from the early volcanoes and of oxygen produced by the first plant life.

Left: Mercury has no atmosphere due to its small size and its proximity to the Sun.

Left: Venus has a dense atmosphere that mainly consists of carbon dioxide. Such density traps the solar heat, considerably raising Venus' surface temperature.

Left: Mars has a thin atmosphere composed mainly of carbon dioxide with traces of oxygen and water vapor.

Below: The atmosphere is the gaseous layer surrounding our planet. If we compare Earth with other planets, we can see that Earth's atmosphere is rather special: the most abundant gases are nitrogen and oxygen, rather than carbon dioxide as is the case in Venus and Mars, or hydrogen as in Jupiter and Saturn. The composition of our present atmosphere is the result of conditions under which Earth was formed and of the evolution of life on the planet.

A liquid surface: the oceans

Seen from outer space, Earth looks different from the rest of the planets because of the intense blue of the oceans. Earth is the only planet whose surface is covered by water in liquid form. This liquid water was produced by the condensation of steam thrown up by the large number of volcanoes that existed during the first stages of the evolution of our planet, when the Earth was very hot.

Among other things, the presence of liquid water on Earth has been vital for the development of life on the planet. The first forms of life appeared on the seabeds, protected from the Sun's intense ultraviolet radiation that enveloped the Earth. When enough oxygen had been given off by the green algae, a layer of **ozone** (a type of oxygen made up of three atoms) was formed in the atmosphere. This ozone layer is what protects the Earth from ultraviolet radiation. After this ozone layer was formed, life could begin to develop on land, away from the protection of the deep waters.

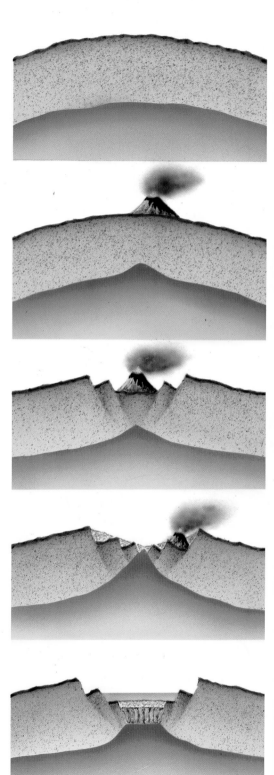

Right: It has been possible to measure the slow movements of the continents. America is moving away from Europe at the rate of a few inches each year. If we imagine this movement in reverse, we can see how, several hundreds of millions of years ago, the continents formed one enormous landmass that we call Pangaea.

Below: The crust is forming continuously at the bottom of the oceans (*left*) and gradually disappears under the continental plates (*right*).

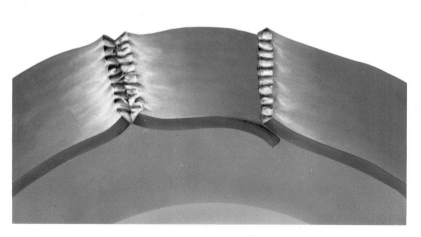

Below: Geologically, the ocean beds are very active areas. In the Atlantic Ocean, for example, there is the mid-Atlantic ridge ① where Earth's interior mantle oozes out to the surface. The hot liquid rock of the mantle solidifies and continually forms new crust on both sides of the ridge. The plates of the crust that support the continents ② are pushed toward each side of the oceans.

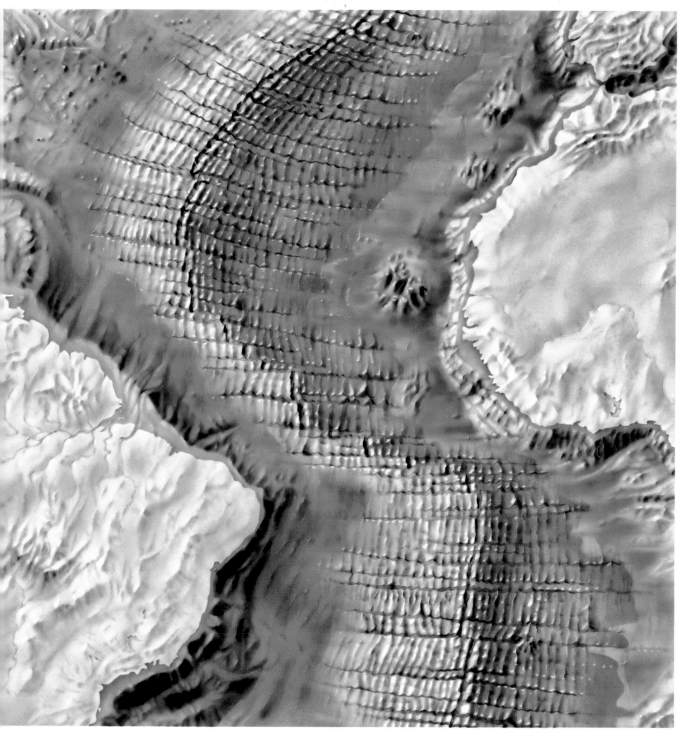

Earth is not isolated

Earth is not a world isolated from the rest of the universe. It is subject to the influence of other stars, and this influence is easily seen. Obviously, the star that has the greatest influence over our Earth is the Sun.

The Sun makes it possible for life to develop and thrive and for human beings to survive on Earth. Sunlight is extremely important to sustain life. The food chain of all living things originated in part from this energy source since plants use sunlight to grow. In addition, all the forms of energy that humanity has at its disposal (except nuclear energy) also come from the Sun including energy from wind and water and from fossil fuels such as coal and petroleum.

Apart from this close relationship with the Sun, the Earth is also inter-related with other bodies of the Solar System, especially the Moon. The Moon is the principle cause of the Earth's ocean tides. The level of the sea rises and falls in a cycle that repeats more or less twice each day. The tides

cause the rotation of the Earth to slow down gradually, and this in turn causes a very slow lengthening of the day.

Left: Earth is constantly showered by meteorites most of which burn up completely in the atmosphere producing shooting stars. Many of these are created when the Earth crosses the orbit of a comet.

Below: The Moon's gravitational attraction is strongest on the near side of the planet. The water closest to it bulges toward the Moon, while the water on the opposite side of Earth forms another bulge. This effect results in the rising and falling of the level of the sea.

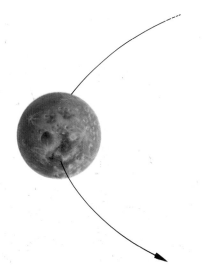
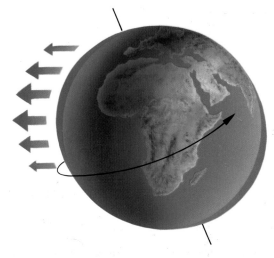

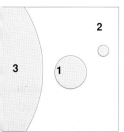

Below: Earth ① has a very close relationship with the Sun ② and the Moon ③. Earth and all the planets were formed by the energy released by the birth of the Sun, the central star of our Solar System. From the Sun, Earth receives all the energy that is necessary to sustain its animal and plant life. The Moon is the principle cause of the ocean tides.

Life beyond the Earth?

Earth is the only place in the universe where we are certain life exists. It is possible that the universe is full of life, but for the moment we have been unable to establish contact with any form of extraterrestrial life. In fact, there has been no definite confirmation of the existence of planetary systems for any star besides the Sun. In our Solar System it is very probable that there is no life anywhere other than Earth. Why has life developed on Earth and not on other planets?

The development of life, as we know it, requires the presence of liquid water or, at least, mild temperatures.

Life exists on Earth because of a delicate balance between the orbit of the planet and the conditions found on its surface. Nevertheless, in developing, life has also been gradually altering these same conditions. Our atmosphere contains oxygen and lacks carbon dioxide as a result of the presence of life on the Earth. Nowadays, humans are capable of altering, voluntarily or involuntarily, this delicate balance. It is our responsibility to keep the Earth habitable.

Below: On Venus, which is closer to the Sun than Earth, the temperature is very high due to the **greenhouse effect**: the carbon dioxide in the atmosphere lets solar light reach and warm the planet, but it does not let the heat escape.

Below: Mars is an example of what Earth would be like if it had been further away from the Sun. Most of the water on Mars is in the form of ice at the polar caps. However, this ice is mostly frozen carbon dioxide, some of which evaporates each summer.

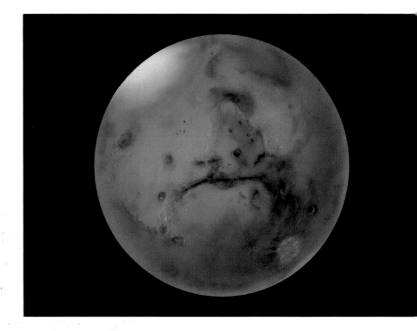

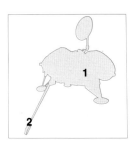

Below: At the moment, it seems that Earth is the only planet in the Solar System where life exists. Mars, the planet that seemed most likely to support life, was explored by two Viking interplanetary probes ① that photographed its surface and took samples of the soil ② to analyze in search of living organisms. The results were negative, and it is expected that this will be confirmed by future explorations.

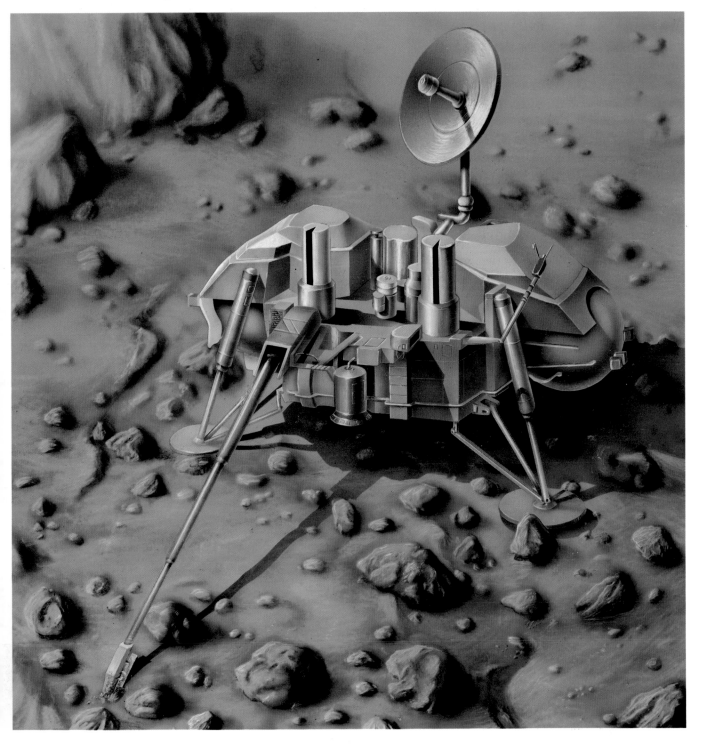

The future of Earth

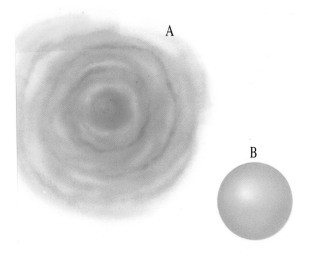

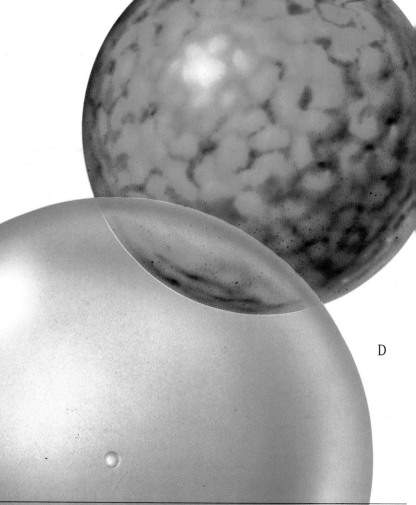

Left and below: Five billion years ago the Sun was born (A). The stability of the Sun in its present phase has made life on Earth possible (B). When the aging Sun becomes a red giant (C) life on Earth will end. Finally, the Sun will shrink as it runs out of nuclear fuel changing into a **white dwarf** (D).

However, from the point of view of astronomy, the future of Earth is very clear. Earth's destiny is closely tied to that of the Sun. In about five billion years, the Sun's energy will start to run out, and it will change drastically to become a **red giant**. The surface of the Sun will swell enormously and thus swallow up the nearest planets. The "end of the world" or at least the end of Earth as a habitable planet is an inescapable fact. Even so, this is not something to worry about at the moment. There are still five billion years to go!

Below: In five billion years' time the Sun will swell and change into a red giant. From the Earth, the Sun ① will appear as a huge reddish sphere that will cover almost the entire sky. The enormous rise in temperature will make the oceans evaporate ②. Earth will become uninhabitable. It is even possible that the planet will be swallowed up by the Sun.

Activity: sundial, our clock from the Sun

The Sun's movement dictates the rhythm of human activity. Until only a relatively short time ago, there was no clock more perfect than the Sun. Nowadays, clocks work with such precision that they even show up the slight irregularities of the Sun's "movement" (it is in fact the movement of the Earth around the Sun that is irregular). Sundials are now used only for decoration and demonstration.

The principle behind the sundial is very simple. Because the Earth rotates, the Sun moves from our view, and seems to turn around the Earth's axis, completing one revolution (360 degrees) every 24 hours. If we align an arm or stick with the angle of the Earth's axis, its shadow will turn in exactly the same way as the Sun. Every hour the shadow will travel 15 degrees, that is to say, one twenty-fourth of 360 degrees. The shadow can be projected onto a flat surface, or dial, which is placed perpendicular (at right angles) to the arm. Lines 15 degrees apart must be drawn on the dial so that each line will represent an hour.

You can make a sundial easily from two pieces of cardboard or thin wood. In this design, the triangular arm part also supports the sundial. The dial part must fit into the arm. The sundial should be placed on the ground facing north so that the arm is pointing toward the North Star (or facing south in the Southern Hemisphere with the arm pointing toward the south celestial pole).

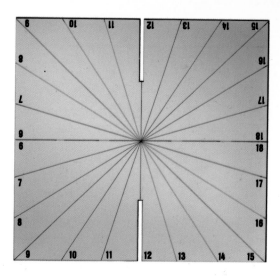

Above: The arm is a triangle in which one of the angles must be the same as the latitude of your location. The dial has two faces, one for winter and the other for summer. Both faces are graduated from 6 to 18 hours (6:00 A.M. to 6:00 P.M.)

Below: The simplest type of sundial can be made by fitting two parts together: the arm and the dial, on which the arm's shadow will be projected. The angle of the triangular arm is equal to the latitude of the location where the sundial is to be used, since it must point to the celestial pole (in the Northern Hemisphere, toward the North Star). The face of the dial must lie perpendicular to the arm, and the entire sundial should be oriented in a north-south direction.

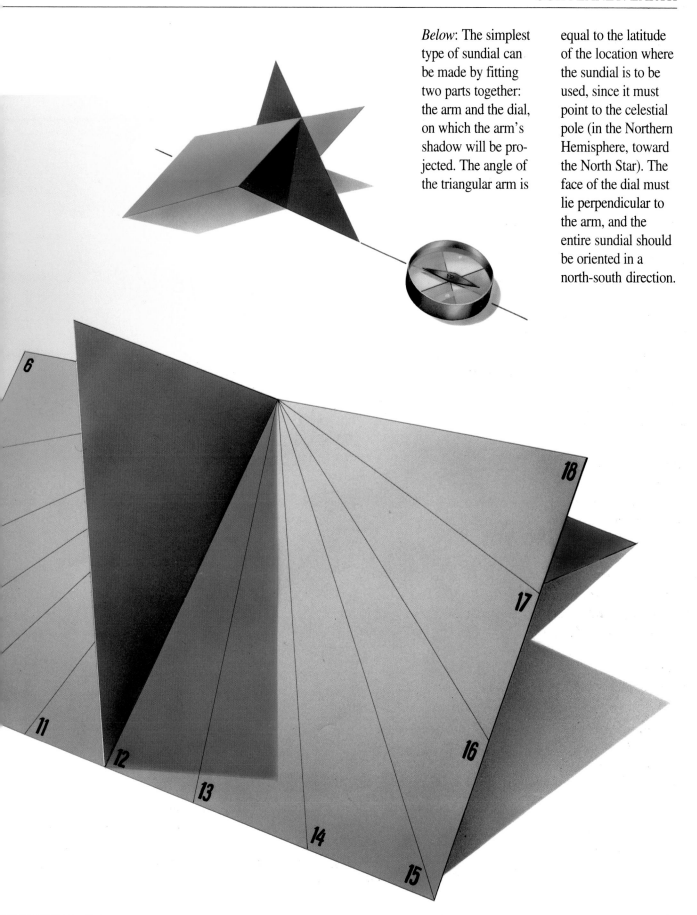

Glossary

atmosphere: The gaseous layer around the Earth consisting mainly of nitrogen (an inert gas) and oxygen.

carbon dioxide: Gas composed of carbon and oxygen present in large amounts in the atmospheres of Venus and Mars. In Earth's atmosphere it only exists in small quantities.

continent: An area of the Earth that has emerged above the oceans and where the crust is especially thick.

continental drift: The slow movement of the continents, which drift a few inches each year.

core: Innermost part of the Earth formed of dense matter such as iron and nickel.

crust: The surface layer of the Earth composed of solid rock.

earthquake: Readjustment of the lowest part of the earth's crust, which produces a disturbance that spreads through the crust in the form of seismic waves. If these are very intense, serious damage to buildings may occur.

equinox: The moment when the spring and autumn seasons begin. The equinoxes occur around March 21 and September 21.

greenhouse effect: A heating process caused by dense cloud cover in an atmosphere. This allows sunlight to reach a planet but traps the resulting heat on the planet's surface.

magnetosphere: The area of interplanetary space where the influence of the Earth's magnetism is felt.

mantle: A part of the Earth's interior beneath the crust, consisting of molten rock.

meteor: A luminous streak that occurs when a particle of interplanetary dust is burnt up on entering the Earth's atmosphere at high speed, also called a *shooting star.*

meteorite: Rock of interplanetary origin that has passed through Earth's atmosphere and fallen on its surface.

oxygen: Gas that forms part of the Earth's atmosphere. It is produced by green plants, and most living creatures depend on it for breathing.

ozone: Form of oxygen composed of three atoms (O_3). It is concentrated in an atmospheric layer over the Earth. The ozone layer absorbs most ultraviolet rays coming from the Sun.

red giant: An old star that has started to cool and has greatly expanded.

silicate: Chemical compound of silicon found in most rocks.

solar wind: Stream of charged particles (electrons and protons) continuously emitted by the Sun and traveling at high speeds throughout the Solar System.

solstice: Moment that marks the beginning of summer and winter. The summer and winter solstices occur around June 21 and December 21.

Van Allen belts: Areas encircling the Earth where the Earth's magnetic field causes an accumulation of the highly charged particles that stream from the Sun.

white dwarf: Star that has consumed all of its internal hydrogen (which is the material that normally allows a star to shine) energy and became small but still shines because it has leftover heat.

ndex

English translation © Copyright 1994 by Barron's
Educational Series, Inc.
The title of the Spanish Edition is *Nuestro Planeta:
La Tierra*

© Copyright 1992 by PARRAMON EDICIONES, S.A.
First edition, May, 1993
Published by Parramón Ediciones, S.A.,
Barcelona, Spain.

Author: Robert Estalella, Professor of Astronomy
Illustrator: Marcel Socías
Consulting Editor for the English edition:
Clinton W. Hatchett, Astronomer

All inquiries should be addressed to:
Barron's Educational Series, Inc.
250 Wireless Boulevard
Hauppauge, New York 11788

Library of Congress Catalog Card No. 93-24597

International Standard Book No. 0-8120-1741-2 (P)
                                                  0-8120-6368-6 (H)

Library of Congress Cataloging-in-Publication Data

Estalella, Robert.
      [Nuestro planeta—la Tierra. English]
      Our planet—Earth / Robert Estalella; illustrated
by Marcel Socías.—1st ed.
          p. cm.—(Window on the universe)
      Translation of: Nuestro planeta—la Tierra.
      Includes index.
      Summary: Describes the earth's formation and its
physical characteristics as well as its relation to
other bodies in the universe. Includes directions for
making a sundial.
      ISBN 0-8120-6368-6.—ISBN 0-8120-1741-2
(pbk.)
      1. Earth—Juvenile literature. 2. Sundials—Design
and construction—Juvenile literature. [1. Earth. 2.
Sundials—Design and construction.] I. Socías,
Marcel, ill. II. Title. III. Series.
QB631.4.E7813 1993
525—dc20   93-24597
                                              CIP
                                              AC

PRINTED IN SPAIN
3456 9960 987654321